THE RIBCHESTER HOARD

BY B. J. N. EDWARDS

Lancashire County Books
1992

The Ribchester Hoard
by B. J. N. Edwards

Published by Lancashire County Books, 143 Corporation Street, Preston
Copyright © B. J. N. Edwards, 1992

First edition, 1992

Typeset by Carnegie Publishing Ltd., 18 Maynard Street, Preston
Printed by T. Snape & Co. Ltd., Boltons Court, Preston

ISBN 1-871236-15-0

The Ribchester Helmet. Reproduced by courtesy of the British Museum.

Aerial photograph of Ribchester, showing the bank of the River Ribble where the Ribchester was found. Reproduced by courtesy of Professor G. D. B. Jones.

THE RIBCHESTER HOARD

O NE day in the summer of the year 1796 a boy was playing in the waste ground at the back of his father's house in the village of Ribchester, on the banks of the River Ribble, some six miles above Preston. His father, who lived in the last house on the right-hand side of the main street of the village as it led down towards the river, was the village clogger.

He was Joseph Walton, and his son, John, was thirteen years old. Exactly what it was that John unearthed as he dug into a hollow we do not now know, but it must have been fairly interesting, for his father came to know of it, and took charge of operations. What they discovered together was a collection of metalwork and other items from the Roman period which, except for the one most important item, has received very little publicity. The single item which has become very familiar to all students of Roman Britain was a bronze helmet.

Whether or not it was the helmet itself which John Walton found first, it is not particularly surprising that father and son went on searching after the first find. They must have been familiar, like all the villagers, with the fact that they lived on the site of a Roman 'station', as it would have been called at the time. Nearly two hundred years had passed since the antiquary, William Camden, schoolmaster and herald, had come that way, enquiring about antiquities, and had noted the villagers' rhyme:

'It is written on a wall in Rome,
That Ribchester was as rich as any
town in Christendom'.

That this rhyme derived from a find long since lost, was first suggested by W. Thompson Watkin in the nineteenth century. When a Roman soldier was discharged from the army he was given, as the equivalent of what we would call today his discharge papers, a pair of bronze plates with holes in their long sides so that they could be held together with a thong. Archaeologists call this a 'diploma'; among other things, a diploma recorded the fact that a tablet, giving the names of the units of the

1

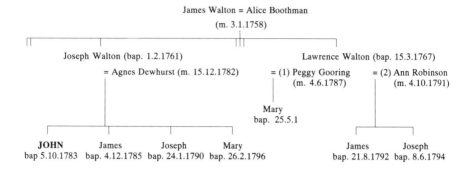

Part of the family tree of the Walton family of Ribchester, based on parish records at the Lancashire Record Office. John, the finder of the hoard, is at the bottom left.

Roman army which were discharging men at the time of its issue, had been fixed on the wall behind the temple of Diana in Rome. It is easy to imagine that such a diploma, discovered in Ribchester, would have been taken to the village priest, whose Latin would have been sufficient to cope with that part of the inscription which was legible and coherent, and would thus lead to the folk memory of roughly what it said.

Camden, collecting material for his book *Britannia* in 1582 and updating it in 1599, was not the first student of the past to visit Ribchester. Of course, the Anglo-Saxon people who gave it a name back in the years before the Norman Conquest, had recognised the remains as those of a fort: after all, 'chester' derived ultimately from the Latin *castrum*. The Saxons, however, left us no other record of their interest in the village's past. Indeed, as far as we know, nor did anyone else throughout the Middle Ages until, as a sideline to one of the great events which define the end of the order of the Middle Ages, John Leland came there.

Leland was given by Henry VIII the task of visiting the monasteries which Henry had dissolved in order to record items of interest there, particularly books. In the quatercentenary of Henry's birth, much has been made of the fact that he was, among other things, a Renaissance scholar. It is to be feared, though, that his interest in the treasures of the monasteries was more in their financial value than in their intellectual importance. Luckily for us, Leland made quite a detailed record of his journeys connected with this task,

2

Frontispiece of Camden's *Britannia*.

and of things which interested him. He came from a family which may have originated in the village of Leyland, but which, by the time of his birth, was living in the vicinity of Leigh. They were poor, and it was only through the generosity of a rich benefactor that John went to St. Paul's School in London. He repaid the trust in his abilities by studying at the universities of Cambridge, Oxford and Paris and ultimately, as we have seen, by attracting the attention of the King – or at least of his advisors.

At Ribchester Leland noted that the inhabitants regularly used to find coins and squared stones. He also recorded a village story – that the Jews once had a temple there. This is interesting,

> DESCRIPTVM · ET · RECOGNITVM · EX · TABV
> LA · AENEA · QVAE FIXA EST·ROMAE
> IN MVRO POST TEMPLVM·DIVI · AVG ·
> AD MINERVAM

The final clause as it might appear on a soldier's certificate of service (*diploma*). Watkin thought that an imperfect memory of the discovery of such an object might have resulted in Camden's 'hobbling ryhme'. The section above, translated, reads: 'Transcribed and examined from the bronze tablet which is fixed in Rome on the wall behind the temple of the Divine Augustus to Minerva'. (Based on the *diploma* found at Malpas, Cheshire, in 1822.)

3

meant that they could build stone houses when others had to be content with wattle, daub and thatch. After the expulsion of the Jews in 1290, there were few, if any, Jews around and the ruins of stone buildings were often ascribed to them. The Jewry Wall at Leicester is a well-known example of a Roman ruin which has, to this day, retained a name linked with the Jews.

After Leland and Camden, we know of few antiquaries who visited the site until the eighteenth century. In the late seventeenth century the village schoolmaster collected objects which were sold by his widow to a Lancashire clergyman on the diocesan staff at Chester. In 1725, William Stukeley came to see the site on his northern journey and Thomas Pennant, traveller and correspondent of Gilbert White of Selborne, also visited it.

By the time the Waltons, father and son, were unearthing their particular find, another clergyman had been showing an interest in Ribchester and its past. He was the Rev. Thomas Dunham Whitaker, whose family had lived at Holme, in Cliviger, for many generations. Whitaker had become incumbent of the family living of Holme Chapel, which he had rebuilt, and was engaged on the first of his series of histories, that of the ancient parish of Whalley, of the parish church of which he was to become vicar in 1809. Whalley, with more than 106,000 acres (over 166 square miles), was the

Bust of John Leland, formerly in All Souls' College, Oxford. From an engraving by C. Grignion.

because it had long been a habit to attribute any unexplained landscape feature to the activities of someone or some group of people who were no longer available to deny it. If it was an earthwork or some other apparently super-human object, it was often attributed to the Devil; if a ruin of a building, to the Jews. It is likely that this results from the fact that Jews, not prohibited like Gentiles from usury, were often very wealthy. This, in turn,

4

The Holme in Cliviger, Whitaker's family home. The chimney pots probably date from after his time. (Engraving, 1974.)

Thomas Dunham Whitaker, 1759–1821. (Engraving after contemporary painting.)

largest parish in Lancashire and, of course, had many chapelries within it. Whitaker, however, was writing the history of the whole ancient parish. We do not know how he came to hear of the Waltons' find. Maybe he came to Ribchester and was told of it, for there was no way in which such a discovery could have been kept secret in a village. Maybe Joseph Walton sought out the man who was known both to be interested in the past and to have influential friends.

By whichever of these means it was, Whitaker heard of the find and through

5

Left (top): Charles Townley
(1737–1805) from a Wedgewood
'cameo' portrait at Towneley Hall.
(Burnley Borough Council).
Photograph by B. J. N. Edwards

Left (below): Townley's house in
Park Street, Westminster (now
Queen Anne's Gate). Photograph
by B. J. N. Edwards

Right (below): Zoffany's painting
of Townley's collection (Towneley
Hall Museum).

Towneley Hall as Charles Townley and Thomas Whitaker knew it. (Engraving after a painting by J. M. W. Turner.)

him, so, too, did Charles Townley. He was then the representative of the family which had lived at Towneley Hall, Burnley, for many years. The family were Roman Catholics and, as such, were denied the outlets for their energies in local politics and administration. As a result, like many another Roman Catholic family, they had forged close links with the continent. In Charles's case, this had led him into collecting classical antiquities, particularly sculpture, and also to his living in London rather than on the family estates in Lancashire. He lived in Park Street, Westminster (now known as Queen Anne's Gate), and his house is marked by one of London's familiar blue plaques.

Within that house he gradually amassed a collection which was open to the public, and which was immortalised in a famous painting by Zoffany, one of the 'society' painters of the day; a

The opening of the manuscript of Charles Townley's description of the find, in the form of a letter to the secretary of the Society of Antiquaries of London, as published in *Vetusta Monumenta*. (Lancashire County Libraries; Harris Library, Preston.)

painting which can be seen today in Towneley Hall Museum, Burnley. Zoffany's picture, in fact, shows a scene which never existed, for objects in the collection which are known to have been distributed around the house are shown in one room.

It must have been a bold step to suggest to Townley that he should buy the Waltons' collection, but buy it he did and, most importantly, he bought all of it – minor objects as well as the helmet.

He then proceeded to do something which he never did with any of the remainder of his collection: he published it, and it is to this publication that we owe our knowledge of exactly what was found.

The standard manner of writing what we should today call an archaeological paper was then in the form of a letter to some official of the society which was to publish it in its transactions. In the case of Townley's report, he was to publish it in a serial publication of the Society of Antiquaries of London called *Vetusta Monumenta*, and his letter was addressed to that Society's secretary, John Brand. Brand was an experienced

8

author, his *History of Newcastle upon Tyne* having appeared in 1789. *Vetusta Monumenta* was a grandiose concept, appearing in parts and surviving to complete only four volumes by 1815. Its page size was 22½ inches by 17½ inches, and it offered scope for the thriving art of engraving, to which its texts were often little more than a commentary.

Townley was able to command the services of James Basire, one of the foremost engravers of the day, to provide four plates; and of these, Basire also executed the drawings for three, the fourth being by Andrea Tendi, an Italian artist. Townley was an exacting client, the proofs of the engravings showing that he had minor features of them altered several times before he was satisfied.

The text which accompanied the plates was replete with the classical learning which we would expect from an educated member of the upper classes in the eighteenth century, and has largely been superseded by more recent research; but there are several interesting aspects of Townley's work in preparing it which are worth looking at.

We can do this because documents relating to its preparation survive in two public collections. First of these is the manuscript of the *Vetusta Monumenta* article itself. This is in the Harris Library in Preston, and is in Townley's own handwriting. It is not a final text,

there being rewritings and new versions of many parts of it. One of these gives us a clue about Townley the author. It will be recalled that he was ostensibly writing to John Brand, the secretary of the Society of Antiquaries. Townley contrived to include a passing reference to Brand's book on Newcastle, and there are three versions of this among the manuscript. In one he refers merely to 'your *History of Newcastle*'; in another to 'your learned *History of Newcastle*'. A third uses the expression 'your much esteemed *History of Newcastle*', and it seems highly probable that the increasing degrees of sycophancy in these references reflect increasing amounts of assistance to the neophyte author, and that many of the other rewritings may have been in response to Brand's suggestions.

The other documents which enable us to see Townley at work are in the library of the Department of Prehistoric and Romano-British Antiquities at the British Museum. Here there is another version of the text of the article, but this time it is the final version almost as printed, and it is not in Townley's handwriting, but in a much neater hand which suggests a professional copyist. The only exception to this is that the quotations in Greek are added by Townley. Presumably the amanuensis was not classically educated. More revealing are a number of other papers. These include a plan, drawn and lettered by Townley, which tells us

9

The helmet as shown in Basire's engraving of his own drawing in *Vetusta Monumenta* (much reduced).

where the find was made. This has never been published, though it would be a routine item to include in a modern report of such a find as that at Ribchester.

Other papers relate to the question of what we should today call restoration. It was commonplace in the eighteenth century, and indeed later, to illustrate damaged objects as though they had been complete, without indicating how much of the illustration was restoration. This Townley rejected. Not only did he insist that damaged parts which had been restored in Basire's engravings should be clearly indicated, but he had an engraving made, almost certainly from a drawing of his own, which was inserted at the end of his text and, the caption tells us, was 'to authorise the reparations shown in the Plate'. Even then the 'reparations' did not include the central portion of the so-called 'diadem' of the helmet, where no evidence survived to show what decoration it had borne.

Townley was tempted. A small sheaf of pencil drawings, pinned together, is among the British Museum papers. They bear a number of possible restorations for that central panel. He was also interested in following up what we would call 'parallels' for other aspects of the decoration of the helmet. Bound with the manuscript at the British Museum are wash drawings of shields and the shapes called *peltae* which are among the decorative elements of the helmet. A further intriguing paper is a sheet torn from a book. It shows various baggage animals as they are depicted on such monuments as Trajan's Column. Among them are camels which have their baggage loaded in panniers which are very similar in shape to two objects shown on the helmet – objects which we cannot identify. It does not seem very likely that these are meant for camel panniers, but Townley was investigating them and, not having the facility of the photocopier which we should use today, did the only possible thing and mutilated the book. Let us hope it was his own.

All this shows that, although constrained by the conventions of his time, Townley's attitude to the antiquities from Ribchester was much closer to our own that we would have expected. It is a great pity that he did not pursue his interest in British antiquities beyond the Ribchester find, and the purchase of the shield boss found at Kirkham about 1800. What he did collect – the Ribchester items, the Kirkham shield boss and the classical sculpture – came to the British Museum after Townley's death, not by will, but by purchase.

If we turn to a consideration of what was found at Ribchester by the Waltons, we discover that about thirty objects were recorded in all. There is reason, as we shall see, to think that at least one of these objects never existed,

11

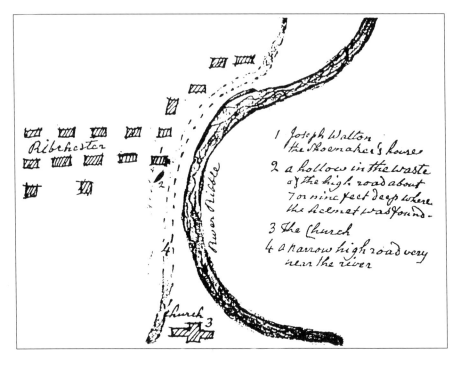

Above: Plan, drawn by Charles Townley, to show the spot where the hoard was
found, marked '2'. (British Museum, Department of Prehistoric and Romano-British
Antiquities.)

Below: Basire's engraving of Charles Townley's own drawing, intended to show how
much of the helmet 'diadem' was restored in the main illustration. (Reduced.)

12

and some of the non-metallic items may have been ordinary finds from the remains of the Roman fort rather than being directly associated with the helmet and horse harness pieces which make up most of the rest of the find. In fact, there are three main elements in the metalwork of the find: first, the helmet; next, the skillets or mess-tins; and finally, the horse harness decorations.

It is obvious that the whole find is to be associated with cavalry. We know already that the fort at Ribchester was garrisoned by cavalrymen. One of its units was almost certainly an *ala* (wing) of cavalry which originated in Asturia. Later, it was occupied by Sarmatian horsemen from what is now Hungary. The size of the fort fits a cavalry garrison of five hundred men, and its commander, in at least one phase of its life, was a former legionary centurion on a normal rung of the promotion ladder as a cavalry prefect.

This takes us to the helmet itself. We are told that among the training carried out by Roman auxiliary cavalry units, parade exercises involving mock battles took place. A helmet such as that from Ribchester would have been used on such an occasion. There is no doubt that the helmet is not a functional one. Not only would it have been silly to use a highly-decorated object in battle but, in addition, it would not have provided much protection, being too thin. Furthermore, while wearing it, one

would have had difficulty in seeing enough to counter the activities of an enemy, and in breathing in the exertion of a fight.

It consists of two parts: the helmet proper, and a face-mask. The latter, also, can be considered in two parts though they are not physically separate. These are the face-shaped part covering the wearer's face and the so-called 'diadem' which covers the wearer's brow and joins face to helmet.

The helmet itself is decorated with fighting men in fairly high relief. They have been raised from the sheet by using a die within the helmet, and one's first reaction is to describe the scene as a battle. Closer examination shows, however, that while seventeen men are shown, all in the process of fighting, they are not actually fighting each other. That is to say, they are disposed haphazardly, and at least one is clearly seated but has nothing on which to sit. One might risk a guess that the dies were designed for a battle scene but have been used almost at random on the helmet. The figures themselves are sometimes naked, sometimes armoured. Some have swords and some spears; some one shape of shield and some another; some are on foot, some mounted. Apart from the not very surprising observation that all the spearmen are mounted, there does not seem to be any correlation between these various details.

The cap part of the helmet has two

13

other decorative elements. On the neck guard are incised a trophy of arms and two *peltae*. We have already seen that the shapes of these attracted Charles Townley's attention. The other decorative element is a mystery. Just above the ears of the helmet, which are partly arranged on the cap partly on the face-mask, are two objects shown in relief like the fighters. They look to modern eyes rather like straw laundry-baskets, tapering somewhat from top to base. Consideration of these brings us to look at other helmets with which to compare the Ribchester example.

At least sixty helmets of the general type we are considering have been recorded from the Roman Empire, the majority of them not far from its frontiers. In one classification, at least, there are only two which compare directly with the Ribchester helmet. One of these was among three helmets found in the course of the excavation of the Roman fort at Newstead in Roxburghshire in the early years of this century. The other comes from Nicopolis on the River Jantra in Bulgaria, and is in the Austrian National Museum in Vienna. The distinctive feature of the type is the slanting raised peak with projections on its edge. The Ribchester helmet has five of these: one round, two in the shape of a palmette and the two nearest to the wearer's eyes in the outline shape of a dolphin. The Newstead helmet has two

and the Nicopolis helmet, one. The decoration of the three helmets is otherwise quite different, Newstead having a scene of a chariot drawn by two leopards and driven by a cupid, and Nicopolis a sacrificial scene. *But* just above the ears of the Newstead helmet are two 'linen baskets' and, in the same position on the Nicopolis helmet there are two ovoid shapes, wider at the top than the bottom, though differently decorated. One attractive suggestion that has been made is that they represent, in the cases of Newstead and Ribchester at least, the stuffed straw dummies into which a trainee cavalryman had to learn to stick his spear while on the move. Even if this interpretation is accurate, however, it is not easy to see why they should be shown on parade helmets.

The face-mask of the Ribchester helmet is in the form of a rather delicately-featured visage. It has been pointed out that it is rather feminine in shape, and it has been suggested that mask and helmet do not, or did not, belong together. The fact that there is at least one other helmet with equally feminine features, but with a moustache, seems to dispose of that difficulty. There is a row of curls shown along the brow, above which is the 'diadem', to which we will turn in a minute. Curls of hair also accompany a representation of a chin-strap down the sides of the face and below the chin. These hair curls turn into snakes' heads.

14

Drawing of the rear of the Ribchester helmet, showing the disposition of the six mounted and eleven dismounted armed figures which make up its decoration, together with the two enigmatic objects over the ears and the *peltae* and trophy of arms on the neck-guard.

15

The 'diadem' is a little difficult to describe. Nearest to the wearer's brow is a wall with eight pepper-box turrets evenly disposed along it, each of them having three round-headed windows. There is a round-headed door between the outermost pair of turrets on each side and a pair of similar doors between the two central turrets. Above the wall, which has crenellations, is an arcade of seven low arches with a cupid's head at each intersection and at the ends, making eight in all. The decoration under these arches varies, but each of the three to one side of the central one is roughly mirrored by its equivalent on the other side. Each of the outermost pair has a twin-tailed merman. Then comes a pair of *putti* or cupids, one resting on a creature with a horse-like head and a serpentine tail, the other on a lump which presumably represents a rock. The next two arches contain inward-facing Victories in flight, carrying palm branches. Finally, the centre arch had entirely gone before Townley acquired the helmet, and Basire's engravings do not restore a decoration, though less wise modern illustrators have done so. So, too, have they shown the helmet part gilded, part silvered, for which there does not seem to be any evidence on the original.

There are two rivets on the centre line of the front of the cap of the helmet, which presumably held an internal hook which would have engaged with a loop on the top of the face-mask. There are also two loops, one not far behind the rivets and the other low down at the back. These may have held some form of crest, though it is not easy to see how they would have functioned. Even more difficult to explain is a small loop low down at the back right of the helmet.

Finally, there are *graffiti*. Today we think of this word in connection with vandalism, but to the archaeologist *graffiti* provide valuable evidence. (Just where the line occurs between these is uncertain. A runic inscription in the church of Santa Sophia in Istanbul is archaeological evidence of Vikings – modern scribbles are vandalism.) At least these Roman *graffiti* had the merits of being both functional and inconspicuous. So inconspicuous were they, indeed, that they were not recorded until as late as 1960. They are punched (i.e. the letters are made up of dots) and they both (there are two) read CARAVI. Presumably this is some form of ownership mark, and it has been pointed out that the only names like them known in the Roman world have been recorded in Spain. Is this evidence for connecting the helmet with the Asturian garrison?

After the elaborations of the helmet, it is a bit of an anticlimax to pass on to consider mess tins. However, there is little doubt that the next three objects in the group were the Roman equivalent of these. They look to us more like small bronze saucepans, and they have the very 'modern' device of concentric

16

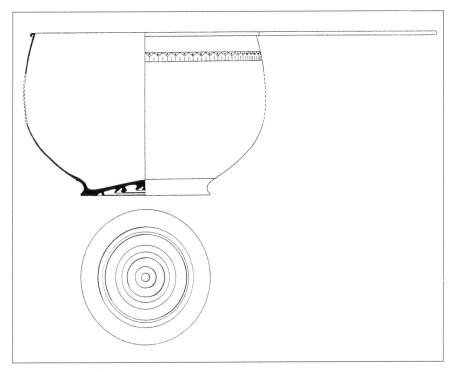

Reconstruction drawing of one of three camp kettles or 'skillets'. The left-hand side is shown as though cut away, to demonstrate the thickness of the metal. There is no general agreement as to the reason for the complex design of the bases of such vessels. Diameter of opening at top of vessel 18cm (7 inches).

rings on their bases to increase their efficiency. One is complete, one is represented by its handle and rim only, and the third by handle, rim and base. One of the handles bears a partially-decipherable maker's stamp, and at the end of their handles all three have holes for hanging them.

Townley next described two items which are slightly curious – a bronze vase and a bronze dish. There is no illustration of these in Basire's illustrations for *Vestuta Monumenta*, but we do have some hint of a shape for the vase in that Whitaker also got Basire to make engravings of the Ribchester finds for his *History of Whalley*, published in 1801. This was presumably done at the last minute, since he did not include any text to go

17

with the illustrations. This lack was supplied only when the book was in its fourth edition, in the 1870s, long after Whitaker's death. Basire shows the vase, which Townley said was represented only by its base and part of its wall, as a fairly ordinary 'flower vase' shape with a narrow neck and quite small rim. Townley, however, also says of the vase that 'the metal has a hue of silver'. When this is taken with the fact that Basire's engraving shows the base of the vase with concentric rings like those of the skillets just described, for which there would be no call on a vase, there is little doubt that the 'vase' is the product of imagination. Whether or not the dish, which Basire shows as a shallow pie-dish shape, really existed, we cannot say. It does not seem to be in the British Museum today, unlike most of the other objects.

It ought to be explained, in case it is thought that there should not be any doubt whether or not the dish is in the British Museum, that the Museum operated rather differently in the early nineteenth century from how it operates today. Were such a find as that from Ribchester to be made now, all its components would, of course, be kept together. When the Museum received Townley's collection, like objects were stored with like, splitting the unity of the Ribchester find. Some objects were marked with a white 'T' for Townley, others were not. It is no small tribute to the Museum's staff that almost all the

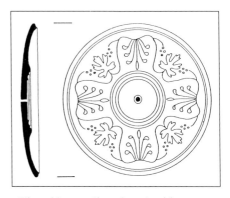

Tinned bronze 'junction-plate' harness mount, with cross-section on left. Loops on rear not shown; probably had a domed rivet in the centre. Diameter 9cm (just over 3½ inches).

Ribchester finds have been relocated.

The next items to be described all formed part of the harness of a Roman cavalryman's mount, which consisted of a number of items held together by straps. Where these straps joined, it was necessary to have some form of 'junction box' into which the straps could be fitted. In practice, these consisted of slightly concave bronze discs with the requisite number of loops on the back, depending on how many straps were joining. The straps themselves had bronze fittings which connected with the loops on the discs. These might be tinned or silvered and were often decorated. Other, smaller discs were located at intervals on some straps, particularly that going round the horse's chest and that round its hindquarters.. These smaller discs had various forms of pendant hanging from them as decoration. In addition, the horse would wear a saddle, usually covered with a saddle cloth, and a head-covering, sometimes metal, sometimes leather, fitted with perforated eye-guards. Some, at least, of most of these features were present at Ribchester.

There were four of the larger type of junction plate, each 3½ inches in diameter, with varying numbers of loops on the back and varying positions for those loops. Basire's engravings had shown these plates as plain and undamaged. In this he was following the normal practice of his day, which Townley had not permitted in the case of the helmet. In fact, all four are damaged today and were almost certainly so when found, but all four are also decorated with incised patterns based on vine leaves and grape bunches, and are tinned. Thus, they are quite elegant and elaborate horse-furniture, without rising to the opulence of the silvered examples such as those found at Fremington Hagg in Yorkshire; still less to that of the silvered set with imperial portraits, found at Xanten in Germany. It is also clear from Basire's engraving that there was originally a boss, held in position by a rivet, in the centre of each disc.

Only a fragment of one of the strap ends, of which examples were also found at Fremington and in many other places, still adhered to one of the loops in Basire's engraving. Speaking of Basire's rendering of these plates raises a curious point. It will be remembered that Basire also engraved the Ribchester finds for Whitaker's *History of Whalley*. When he came to the harness plates (neither he nor Townley knew what their function was, and called them *phalerae*), he showed them as a series of four in graduated sizes. Since he must have known that they were all the same size, this is odd, but it may be explained by another of Townley's sketches in the British Museum. In this case, he was looking at illustrations of signifers (standard-bearers) and at least one form of *vexillum* or standard does have a number of graduated discs on its shaft.

There were also three smaller discs, each 1¾ inches in diameter, also decorated but with the remains of two

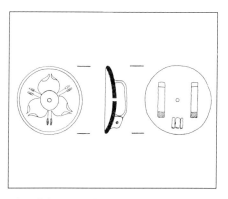

Small harness plate.

19

vertically-set loops on the back. These would have adorned a strap, but not at a junction, and would have had a pendant hanging from them. This type of pendant was also found at Fremington and at other sites such as the fort at Newstead already mentioned in connection with the helmet. Next we come to some objects which are not readily explicable. These were four thin circular bronze plates, rather damaged, but almost certainly having a number of rivet holes near their edges. Apart from saying that they look like the backing for something now lost, little can be said about these.

That is not so when we come to the next part of the Waltons' find. These were one complete small bronze hemispherical object with a pattern perforated through it, and parts of two other similar objects. They looked a bit like small bowls, and Townley called the complete one a '*colum* or colander'. If they had indeed been colanders, they would have been for straining very small objects; but Townley did not have the advantage given to us by later finds. Once again it is Newstead which comes to our rescue. Here was found a leather shape which was shown to be designed to cover the front of a horse's head. Called a 'chamfron' or 'chamfrein', it was decorated with a pattern executed in bronze rivets, and the eye-holes were the right size for our Ribchester 'colanders'. This, then, is what they were: eye-guards from a horse harness.

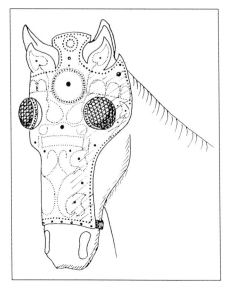

Sketch of the head of a horse wearing a leather chamfron like that from Newstead, with bronze eye-guards based on those from Ribchester. No upper strap is shown because there is no evidence of where it was attached.

Other examples of these have been found on the continent, often with bronze plates rather than a leather base, but a chamfron very like that from Newstead has fairly recently been found at Vindolanda, near Hadrian's Wall.

It will be remembered that the *graffiti* on the helmet suggested a link with the Asturian garrison. The chamfron, on the other hand, makes us wonder about the Sarmatians who were certainly heavy-armed cavalry. They are shown

20

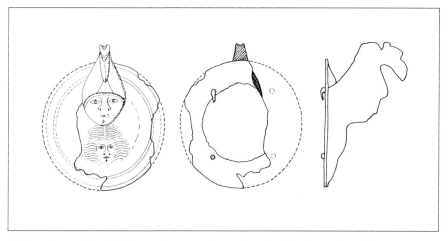

Three views of a gilded bronze harness decoration showing the goddess Minerva
wearing a helmet and the Gorgon's head breastplate. Diameter of mount 7cm (nearly
3 inches.

on Trajan's Column in Rome, by an
artist who must have been working
from a description rather than personal
knowledge, as covered in fish-like
scales – horses and all – and a
tombstone at Chester seemed to have
had a similar carving. It is possible that
a chamfron was once discovered at
Ribchester. Whitaker records that there
was a story in the village of the finding
of an ox's skull covered in leather and
studded with gold. Now an ox's skull
and a horse's do not appear very
different to the layman, and the damp
conditions which would have preserved
the skull, and which we know to be
fairly common at Ribchester, might
well have preserved the rivets in their
·original golden colour, just as many

coins came out of water-logged
deposits at Carlisle as bright as on the
day they had been lost.
    Only three metal objects of the
Ribchester hoard remain to be
described, and we can dismiss one of
these right away. This was what
Townley thought to have been a bronze
candelabrum; two pieces of this
survived, but since he did not illustrate
them or describe them further, we
cannot relocate them in the British
Museum or comment further. This
leave us with, first, a small bronze bust
which Townley identified as Minerva.
It is damaged, but what remains of the
fittings on the back show that it is again
a piece of harness-decoration, and the
centre of a chest-strap would be an

21

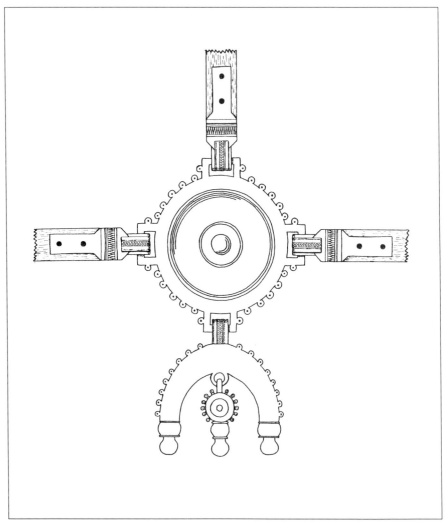

Reconstruction drawing of a harness mount and pendant. Enough of the central element and of one of the strap terminals survive to make that part of the reconstruction certain. The central element is concave, and has here been supplied with a bossed plate to cover it. The terminals and the small central part of the lower pendant are imaginary, but based on other examples. Diameter of central roundel 8.5cm (3¼ inches).

22

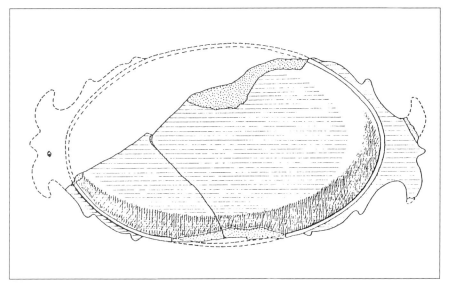

Drawing of a shale dish, restored from fragments found at Ribchester in 1974. A dish of this type may have been found with the 1796 hoard. This dish was about 250mm (9¾ inches) long and 123mm (4¾ inches) wide.

appropriate position for it. The final object of the three completely baffled Townley and Basire. What they had was a concave bronze disc with loops on its edge and two smaller pieces which seemed to belong to it. Basire produced a reconstruction of a sort of circular buckle with four similar circular objects disposed around it. Again, study of recent research on horse harness shows it to be another variation on the theme of a strap-distributor and pendant decoration.

The non-metallic objects which Townley lists in his publication were three in total: a *mortarium*, or pottery mixing bowl; a boar's tusk; and a wooden object. The mixing bowl is slightly unusual in being complete and undamaged. It is stamped by a potter working in the Calais area at the end of the first century AD and, if it really belongs with the metalwork, is the most closely dateable object in the group. But it may not belong. It would have been possible to conceal the smaller metal objects in it, or to use it as a lid for a larger pottery vessel which was broken by the finders – *mortaria* are strong and not easily broken. The boar's tusk must surely be an accidental find. It is shown in Basire's engraving for Whitaker, but his editors in 1872 did not recognise it and called it 'a sickle-shaped object'. The wooden object was listed merely as a piece of wood ten inches long and having a mortice hole. In both handwritten versions of the text, however, it is joined by another object. In the original Preston manuscript this is described as 'a part of a flat wooden dish with the appearance of a small moulding at the edge of it'. But in the British Museum manuscript, which is almost certainly the printer's text, it has become 'A flat piece of wood, so decayed, as to leave no room for conjecture relative to its use'. Finally, it was left out of the printed version, and we may wonder whether this again shows the influence of John Brand. As to its identity, the original description would fit one of the flat shale dishes of which an example was found at Ribchester in 1974.

The last item which formed part of John and Joseph Walton's find has been dealt with last because it had been lost even before Townley bought the remainder. Whitaker who saw it, said that it was a sphinx, and that its base was curved and had solder on it. He thought it might have been fixed on the top of the helmet, which is improbable, but gives us some idea of how big it was. It had been given to Lawrence Walton, who was the brother of Joseph and a calico weaver. It had then been lost by his children, Joseph, who was about eight years old, and Mary, half-sister to Joseph, two years old.

What does this discovery, made almost two hundred years ago, tell us about life at Roman Ribchester? What made a cavalryman conceal his treasured parade helmet, his camp mess-kit and the decorations of his horse's harness? The short answer to this is, of course, that we can never know. We cannot really date the concealment at all closely. Art historians seem to agree in dating the helmet to the late first century AD. The remaining harness fittings are not closely dateable, though the *mortarium*, for what it is worth, seems also to be from the late first century. Only the hint of a connection with the Sarmatians would go against this, for we have no evidence that any Sarmatians were in Britain, never mind at Ribchester, before 175AD. Quite apart from this, all one can say of the concealment of any hoard of objects in the ground is that it took place later (much or little later) than the date of manufacture of the latest item in the hoard. As we can see, we have little to go on. We can, however, deduce at least two points of interest from the find. First, it enables us to visualise a little more clearly the daily life of the cavalry whose duty it was to garrison the fort. They were not just workaday soldiers, but they had their days of finery and display. Secondly, it suggests to us something of the insecurity of their lives. They may have come from anywhere in the Roman Empire, but they were certainly far from home. They were on an island which their geographers had not long since said ought not to exist. And their very presence indicated that they were in potentially hostile territory. It is fairly easy for us to imagine, on a misty day in the wild country where Hadrian's Wall runs, the possibility of an enemy band looming out of the murk. Such fancies are less easy in the comparative lushness of the Ribble Valley today, but they must have been just as real when one cavalryman hid his treasured possessions – perhaps before going out on patrol – for a small boy to find over one and a half millennia later. And spare this thought, too: that these objects were there to be found, presumably means that the soldier's direst forebodings were justified. He never returned to claim them.

Bibliographical Note

The objects found at Ribchester in 1796 and bought by Charles Townley were published by him in the Society of Antiquaries' periodical publication *Vetusta Monumenta*. The section of Volume IV which contained the Ribchester article was published in 1800, though the complete volume is dated 1815. Illustrations of some of the objects were included in all four editions of T. D. Whitaker's *History... of Whalley* . . . (1800–1801, 1806, 1818, and 1872–1876) with explanatory notes added only in the last. A full account will appear shortly in *Ribchester Excavations*, Part 4, edited by B. J. N. Edwards and P. V. Webster. The line illustrations in this booklet are all newly drawn from the objects themselves by the author.